Doctor Placebo

Also by Alan Wall:

Poetry
Jacob
Chronicle
Lenses
Gilgamesh
Alexander Pope at Twickenham

Fiction
Curved Light
Bless the Thief
Silent Conversations
The Lightning Cage
The School of Night
Richard Dadd in Bedlam
China
Sylvie's Riddle

Non-fiction
Writing Fiction
Myth, Metaphor and Science

Doctor Placebo

Alan Wall

Shearsman Books
Exeter

Published in the United Kingdom in 2010 by
Shearsman Books Ltd
58 Velwell Road
Exeter EX4 4LD

www.shearsman.com

ISBN 978-1-84861-133-7
First Edition.

Copyright © Alan Wall, 2010.

The right of Alan Wall to be identified as the author of this work has been asserted by him in accordance with the Copyrights, Designs and Patents Act of 1988.
All rights reserved.

Acknowledgements

'Ruskin and Sesame' was first published in *Shearsman*; 'Trivium', 'Labyrinth' and 'Origin of Species' were first published in *Temporel* (with translations by Anne Mounic); an earlier and shorter version of 'Doctor Placebo' was first published in *International Literary Quarterly*.

Contents

Part 1: Doctor Placebo

The Doctor	11
DIY	12
Placebo's Relics	13
Oculist Placebo	14
Now He Attends to the Blind	15
One of the Doctor's Favourites	16
Placebo Astray	17
Placebo Divided	18
Placebo Dreams of Rome	19
In the Library	20
Bereft in Turin with Brother Friedrich	21
Moonman Placebo	23
Placebo Elegiac	24
Snicker-Snack	25
History turns Personal	26
Religio Medici	27
Placebo's Tinnitus	28
Placebo's X-ray	29
Placebo's Winter	30
Placebo in Mufti	31
Placebo's Dreamroom	32
Mirror-Phase	33
Origin of Species	34
The Drinking Philosopher	36
Placebo's Palimpsest	38
Placebo's Music Hall	39
His Bafflement	40
Revenant	41
Prognosis	42
Hemispheric Consolations	43
The Square on the Hypotenuse	44
Doctor Placebo and Doctor Johnson	45
Religio Medici #2	46

The Ring	47
Placebo's December	51
Bibliophile Placebo	52
Fittest	55
Placebo Thinks Darkly of John Ruskin	56
20th Century Elegy	57
Placebo's Guardian Departs	58
Insomniac Placebo	59
Placebo's Lifeline	60
Imitation of Life	61
Placebo's Midrash	62
Placebo Pedagogical	63
Placebo and the Entrails	64
Placebo's Forebear	65
Bonjour Placebo	66
Placebo Under the Sign of Saturn	67
Placebo's Last Orders	68
Part 2: Ruskin and Sesame	71
Part 3: Labyrinth and Trivium	85

To

Ann and David Denham

PART ONE

DOCTOR PLACEBO

The Doctor

1

Doctor Placebo was asked
If he could vouchsafe
One true thing at least.

I have abandoned certainties, he said
Or perhaps they have abandoned me.
The speed of light remains constant
In a vacuum, of that I am reasonably certain
Though disproof is still possible
At the unreached edges of the universe.

And there's mortality, of course.

Charles Péguy remarked in *Clio*
That History constitutes dark reflections
Upon falling things.
Shortly afterwards History assassinated him
For this impertinence.

DIY

Placebo operated on himself
Several times.

These manoeuvres at least
Alerted him to the heart's attentiveness
When probed.

Its red alert on encountering
A foreign body.

He also acknowledged at last
(As he administered rigorous post-operative care)
The value of accurate stitching,
An art he had once thought
Merely womanish.

Placebo's Relics

Medieval remnants of the true cross
Marilyn's dress

A fragment of James Dean's last car
Elvis's guitar

An image, however contrived, of the Cottingley Fairies
The Hitler Diaries

A first edition of *Sigmund Freud: Collected Works*
Pip and Joe Gargery's larks

A photograph of Eva Braun's false teeth
Propped up by the Hippocratic Oath

Oculist Placebo

In *La Bête Humaine* Severin says to Jean Gabin:
'Don't look as hard as that at me:
You'll wear your eyes out.'
And when Leo Stein handed his book of engravings
To the youthful Pablo Picasso, the Spaniard
Stared so fiercely at them, Leo declared
Himself surprised there was anything left on the page
Once he'd finished.

One of my patients peered at me anxiously
Awaiting my diagnosis.

'It's a pathogenic metaphor,' I announced
'Which has taken over your life.
'It's all you'll ever see now
'Even with the curtains drawn and your eyes closed.'

Now He Attends to the Blind

Like Gloucester in *King Lear* or Milton
My patient underwent the gnosis of a blinding.
Eyeless then in Gaza or in Chalfont St Giles,
On the road to Dover, up against
The sweatstink of an evil hearth
Or merely Placebo's book-lined surgery in Bermondsey
The blind speak Tiresias's lingo, the sightless
Orienteering of the seer.

Hölderlin thought Oedipus's crime
Was to stare into the darkness of the gods,

Their *nefas*. Thus did he answer the Sphinx's riddle
Guaranteeing his self-blinding later.

One of the Doctor's Favourites

When Doctor Placebo considered Spinoza
He witnessed a man grinding lenses
In the age of lenses.

Staring into the glass he saw
The Milky Way (unspeakably vast)
Through another lens he saw a flea
Its armadillo armour articulating
Movements through a microcosmic world.

Through the last lens he ever ground
Glass sedimenting his lungs
He saw God, in all the glory
Of His quantum states
With only the mildest hint
Of chromatic diffraction.

Placebo Astray

A minute cloud in the left-hand corner of a sky
Otherwise insultingly blue

The beach is a Möbius Strip, neverending
As you flip the mind first this way then that

I think a shark appeared yesterday salted with composure
While I sat dryly here

And last night I woke badly from a dream
In which an old enemy, a successful sailor, called me Robinson

From the prow of his boat and shouted
'Do you never open your emails any more?'

Placebo Divided

Felipe II, inside the palace, surrounded by
The most voluptuous flesh available in Europe
In the form of Titian's paintings, had his suit of armour
Erected outside in the courtyard to survey his troops.

That suit of armour was Doctor Placebo
Prognosticating and prescribing to a queue
Of uniform diseases and complaints,
Quotidian pathologies, while behind closed doors
A poet scribbled, in the centre of the harem
Art legally affords us.

The metal suit was what the world paid for
And saluted.
His poems he provided free.

Placebo Dreams of Rome

Smoke on that hill up there has smutched the sky.
A village, probably. Our soldiers in drink
Are merry now. They'll have knifed all the men,
Be having the women, whom they'll have again
Shortly, tears making the coitus a trifle
Salty. But they are salary men
And so must credit themselves
Whenever payment is offered
Or taken.

In the Library

Open on Placebo's lap, Johnson's Dictionary.
His eye rests on 'obstupefaction':
'The act of inducing stupidity, or interruption of the mental powers.'
Now how on earth, he thinks, did that one fall out of use?
Surely its relevance increases every decade.
To think otherwise you'd need to be a fopdoodle:
'A fool; an insignificant wretch.'

And I, Placebo thinks, am a mooncalf:
'A monster; a false conception : supposed perhaps
Anciently to be produced by the influence of the moon.'
Though Johnson's second definition's this:
'A dolt; a stupid fellow.' Both true
Depending on the hour, the day, the month.

When Nicolas Hartsoeker gazed through his microscope
At human sperm what he saw were a myriad homunculi
Tiny men curled up inside the foetus of their cells,
The last a word bequeathed to us by Robert Hooke
Who, staring at a slice of cork through magnifying lenses
Was reminded of a honeycomb: 'little bags or bladders,
Where fluids, or matter of different sorts are lodged.'

Yet they had no trouble delivering children.

Bereft in Turin with Brother Friedrich

Ressentiment:
Motor of history, according to Nietzsche.
The slave resents the master
The loser the winner
While the thinker in the Age of Chaos
Resents everything, most of all himself
Whom he loathes for not becoming a person
Merely a rendezvous of personalities.

One diagnosis in three, if Placebo had been honest
Which doctors can seldom be.
Resentment: it chills the blood
Reverses the affections
Turning the sweet smell of life to acrid stink.

Instead the Doctor in his surgery treated them in turn for
Migraine depression dyspepsia alcoholism bad backs
Insomnia bulimia anorexia
All forms of metaphoric sorrow.

Accept your illness, Nietzsche said,
It will not leave you now.
Accept this long disease your life.
What does not kill me strengthens me.
Russian fatalism, he called it, lying down in the snow
Smiling at what is ordained:
Winter and its chill provisions.

Accept your deformity, cripple.
Celebrate your agony. You are lucky.
We are small diseases
Loving our victims.

2

In January 1889 at the age of forty-five
He collapsed in Turin
His arms around the neck of a horse
Which had just been whipped.

Seven years earlier when thirty-eight
He had been photographed harnessed to a cart
Together with his friend and devotee Paul Rée.
Sitting in the cart is Lou Andreas-Salomé
Who attracted the unconfined
Devotion of both men
(Plus Rilke; plus Freud).
She is holding a whip and appears very happy
To be holding it.

Friedrich Nietzsche in *Human, All Too Human*:
'Going to visit a woman? Take your whip.'

He lived his words.
His life, it seems, became an allegory;
His work the emblem book.

Moonman Placebo

The moon watches
With her one bandaged eye she stares
From the graveyard where the yew tree salutes.
In an attic high above ground
A poet's foul papers are being sorted.

These might be Placebo's Collected Works.

And turning the pages he recalls
How one of his patients swallowed the moon.

Now her own face was pockmarked
Tarnished and battered like that toothless old bitch
With her ageless grin, in the doorway of the dark up there.

And how did Doctor Placebo help?

He gazed on her features in silence
And thought of Galileo
Eye pressed up against his telescope
Staring at the ruins of the heavens
In the moon's poxed face.
Sidereus Nuncius. 1610.
So swallow this moon in the shape of a white pill each day
Before meals, preferably.

We could call it a lunar placebo.

You must learn how to let the queen of dark regions
Cure you now of all distempers
As I have learnt to do, returning each day to the blank
White face of her pages.

Placebo Elegiac

From what shall he build himself an elegy?
Are they made of anything but words?
Clio traces her finger in the dust,

The Goddess of History's *ipsissima verba*.
Her memories. Her words.
Such are the elementary particles, the standard model

All lords of utterance must utilise
While constructing a universe.
In Osip Mandelstam the age has a broken back.

The slow creature's bright eyes
Are staring down a snowstorm. Eating crystals
Where its disappointed maw had wanted flesh.

Snicker-Snack
i.m. Antoine Lavoisier

Air, you said,
Divides into two:
'Mephitic' and 'highly respirable'.

And you divided into two
When Madame Guillotine let fall her blade;
Lopped off that handsome head
So full of progress and enlightenment.

1794.

The rigorous husband of our sharp madame,
Robespierre, sea-green incorruptible,
Bent to the same razored fate
A moment later. A head disconnected
From the body
Makes intake of the substance problematical.

Oxygen, you called it.

History Turns Personal

Each morning Placebo views his face in the mirror
With growing astonishment. One more return
Against the odds. He has stopped buying
Green bananas. Ripeness is all.

He is starting to know
How Rome must have felt towards the end.

Each grinning face out on the street
Announcing another battle lost,
Another general queasy at his homecoming.

Religio Medici

One of my Russian patients said
She had to kiss an icon every day.
But I'm not one, I said.
You'll have to do. You write poetry
And fathom palpitations of the heart.
Your auscultation fathoms my depths.
So why tremble, Doctor, like a panicked squirrel?
Stay still, she said
Lie back
Don't quarrel.

And a nun came to consult me once.

Beneath the vastness of her black robes
A woman dwelt. Flesh white as milk.

I never could see a full-body X-ray
Without thinking of the Turin Shroud:
'Wrap up well if you think you're dead.'
Survive death the Röntgen way.

Placebo's Tinnitus

A curious hissing in my mind today.

A landscape of grass and rust.
One dead bell
Smashed by the latest Einsatzgruppen
Despatched with sealed orders from the *imperium*.

Inside my head, snakes mating.
I see the turquoise mask
Of the god Quetzacoatl.
One head at both ends.
Both poisonous presumably.

The snakes survived by going underground.
For millions of years they thrived down there
Drawn back finally
Into sunlight's kingdom, this desert where
Each shadow represents a tiny graveyard
And every graveyard's filled with food.
A loud ticking at noon.
The merest movement underneath a spider's rock.

Placebo's X-Ray

Yesterday I spotted a birdcage dumped in a skip
Painted white once , but the paint
Had blistered. Much of it rusted,
The wire door broken off.
I stared up at the sky as if expecting
A late visitor, one who might fly in to choose
Such a locus of decay, a rent-free winter domicile.

Placebo's Winter

The river is locked.
Cold turned the key.
Ice fitted crystal slates
White blue
Blue white.
Blabbermouth water
Censored by seasonal command
Chilled at last into *omertà*.

Now fish have a roof over their heads.

Placebo in Mufti

There was a scent. Its history
He didn't know. Like a contagion
Requiring a specific location, it had attached
Itself to her.

I can diagnose this, he said. I'm a professional
(Pressing a hand to her breast)
I have the requisite qualifications, he said.
I understand from the principles of natural philosophy
Why such a scent should apply so adhesively
To the little acre of your flesh.

Isomorphs at work.
We'd best look into it.

Placebo's Dreamroom

Only in my dreams do you unfasten.

White flesh vivid and untouchable.

Ectoplasm at a séance.

Mirror-Phase

Montezuma stared into his obsidian mirror
And saw there darkness gathering.
Time turning its back on the Aztecs
A future filled with malformed prodigies.

Someone has been tampering with Placebo's mirror:
Its mercury back this day has turned obsidian.

Origin of Species

'A whole cold breakfastless hour on the properties of rhubarb.'
Thus Charles Darwin recalled Andrew Duncan's
Winter lectures on *materia medica*.
One vivid apprehension in the morning frost:
The swish of his mother's black velvet gown.
Her mortal remains lay in St Chad's Church, Montford.

Collector of birds' eggs, minerals, seals, coins
Shooter of gamebirds by the skyfull.
The word about the place was this: rocks
Were sedimentary precipitates, so time
Was fingering the edges of eternity. Colonial flora
Itemised for East India Company men
Who needed their herbal resources out there
Amongst the gallimaufry races.

Meanwhile surgery (minus anaesthesia)
Elicited nausea. During an operation
On a screaming child in the Royal Infirmary
He fled.

Degreeless, with a deep detestation of medicine
Darwin left Edinburgh. April, 1827.
Thence to Cambridge;
Years of avid beetle collecting in the Fens.

John Edmonstone, freed slave from Guiana
Taught him the art of stuffing birds.

The Galapagos Islands were full of them.
Black volcanic rock
Awaited the prow of the Beagle.
Finches with varying lengths of beak

Flapped away their tiny intervals
Till Darwin raised his barrel to the sky.

The Drinking Philosopher

Placebo drinks and is silent.

On his lap a beloved volume.
Ethics by Spinoza.

God is none of the following things
Says Spinoza:

Black white green yellow blind sighted
Father mother
Male female
Loving hateful
Bright dark rainbow quantum
Choosing abstaining
Living dying.

The world's the world
It's everything that is the case.

Vagina
Penis inside vagina
Spermatozoa ovum
Life after that
Or not.

God expresses

Through a massive grammar of invention
Articulate thusness—

Nothing He never says
Nothing—

But then if He did
Placebo reflects
We wouldn't hear Him.

Placebo's Palimpsest

Dawn mist has made the land a palimpsest.

The Gothic doodle of a church spire
Amongst hesitating trees—
Upright letters fled from a vanished language.
Dry stone walls like refugees
From every line in Euclid's *Principles*.

Ponds catch sunlight
Misshapen golden guineas
On the steam laundry floor
Liquid eyes
Earth evolved only this morning.

Telegraph poles signposts pylons
Rigging for ancient ships
Whose decks dissolved centuries ago into the moist *grisaille*.

A crow risks its black heart floating through such inkwash
Anthracite feathers dissolving to milk.

As for the sheep:
White breathing of a wool parenthesis
Grey impossibilities
Erasures
Second thoughts before green gets started.

Placebo's Music Hall

My voice, he thought,
Is an ensemble instrument.
Left alone it starts to sound like Pascal's reed
Not Pan's.

Perhaps I always made my best noise
Contrapuntally in dialogue.

'You're fine. Nothing to worry about.
I don't want to see you again in
Here for a long time.'

He sits in his empty surgery
Staring at flayed anatomies
On his wall.
Those we see right through
We don't see at all.

Röntgen's transcendence expresses itself thus:
Electrons and protons are the ones to break free.

I am my own X-ray.
I've stared so far inside myself
Something stares back
In merciless lucidity
I must try to delineate.

The skull beneath the skin.

What is true now
Was true before:
It's the old standards
Set the crowd on a roar.

His Bafflement

After practising on so many bodies
And creating a *corpus* of his own
Placebo has at last concluded:
Life is not soluble in rationality.

Revenant

Magnifos flit across the grey screen of his mind
Before exiting for ever.

It seems to Placebo that he is turning
Into a graveyard.

Is he the revenant then?
Or are they?

At dawn sometimes he witnesses dark ceremonies
Conducted in a tongue he's never spoken

Hears elegies to make a grown man weep
For lives as yet unstarted.

Once he saw a young man in black, a mourner,
And recognized at once his own pale face.

It was snowing. The snow and sky together were a mirror.
Mercury inside its glass snaked down to zero.

Prognosis

Noting as so often
Nature's little drolleries
He listens to the man in his surgery explain:
'But I only retired six months ago.'

That won't halt its progress, I'm afraid.

Hemispheric Consolations

He has an eirenic nature
But prefers aggression to charm
The former disclosing a hint of truth
While the latter's fit only for courtiers and eunuchs.

Doctor Placebo has discovered
His own grand principle of conservation:

> Whatever I swallow
> Makes me equally well
> Equally ill
> Equally full
> Equally hollow

One final book may be fomenting inside me:
Ending for Beginners.

The Square on the Hypotenuse

Placebo had been brooding once more on Pythagoras.
How they hurried the one errant mathematician amongst them
On to a boat. He had discovered an irrational number
Which threatened the Brotherhood's existence
As surely as the unresurrected bones of Jesus
In Joseph of Arimathea's sepulchre
Would have put paid to early resurrectionists.
He chatters happily, as he had in town
Talking there to those excluded from the Privilege
Of a realm of numbers never yet envisaged,
Nightmarish asymmetric unresolved.
Now here on the boat his gleeful laughter enters their ears
Like the venomous tongue of a snake.

Once far enough out on the water
Away from the eyes of the unenlightened and innumerate,
They took their oars and beat him
To a bloody mass, then heaved his body
Overboard, to go take a tally of the fishes.

He drowned, they say,
Though irrational numbers would soon resurface.

Doctor Placebo and Doctor Johnson

How it concentrates a man's mind
The journey in the tumbril to the *tricoteuses*.

Thus do they come, to attend the sharp falling
Blade of my prognosis.

I smile, consider, touch the affected part
Playing mumchance to this ancient mystery,

As though they each of them were scrofulous,
I the anointed healer of the King's Evil.

The needles click click click
And every afternoon amasses its statistics.

Religio Medici #2

She sent me a handful of dust
From her favourite urn.
I counted it out, grain by grain.

A few years still to go then.

Staring in a pet shop window the next day
I saw vivid images: primeval swamps, the Book of Genesis,
Fresh fossils in the making.
Bought a budgerigar and called it Methuselah,
But he died young
Weighed down by the burden of hope
In the four weighty syllables
I had bestowed upon him.

I buried the bird in the garden
Where I now keep the urn.

The Ring

Charlemagne in old age fell for a girl
Whose name has not been recorded.
Counsellors, courtiers, war-advisors, priests
All were appalled. Affairs of state were neglected.
The Holy Roman Emperor might have been
Neither Holy nor Roman, nor in truth
In charge of an Empire, but his timetables were full in those days,
    even so.

What to do?
Hands were raised, palms outward
Shoulders shrugged.

Europe was already sprinkled with the old man's offspring
From concubines, wives, sundry women who could claim neither
    title.
Now here was another, young enough to be his granddaughter.

Then Nature resolved what courtiers couldn't.
The young girl died, suddenly, without explanation.

The courtiers sighed.
One even laughed for a second
A sound soon smothered with a diplomatic cough.

Now at last the crown would return to its business
Staring with narrowed eyes up the hour-track,
Appeasing the future.

One by one they fell silent as they watched:
The old man had the girl embalmed
Carried in state to his chamber

There to lie beside him every night.
It was said in the dark there were voices.

Archbishop Turpin stepped forth.
Suspecting an enchantment, he demanded a minute examination
Of the deceased. This he performed
In all the dignity of his garments.
Starting with the toenails, he made his way up to the scalp.
Then beginning again with the scalp, made a painstaking journey
All the way back to the toenails.
En route he checked the budding breasts
No infant mouth would ever clamp on now,
And the *mons* with its tiny pubic copse of concealment.
The old man would doubtless have entered that thicket
Before long, had things turned out differently
Which things, of course, never do.

One baffled archbishop. Finally, as an afterthought,
He opened her mouth and lifted up the tongue.

There it was. A gold ring bearing
      at its centre
a perfect globe of lapis lazuli.
(Now lapis is known to facilitate
Communication between the living and the dead.
Placebo himself has had a tiny egg made out of it,
Which he carries around in his pocket at all times.
No voices from the other side as yet
But there's still a little time left.)

Turpin bore the ring in triumph to the courtiers
And as he held it up before them
Like a gleaming monstrance
Charlemagne appeared, walked through the room

Threw his arms around the bulky prelate
And said, 'I love you, Turpin. Always have.'

Bearer now of the agent of enchantment
Turpin found his predicament troublesome.
The status of his office, the dignity of his person,
Both under imperial siege.
Charlemagne followed him everywhere, even to the chapel
Where he went to pray, murmuring,
'Turpin, I adore you. Be mine at last.'
At night the Holy Roman Emperor would bang
Upon the presbytery door
Demanding entrance to the ecclesial bed.

Unable to bear it longer
The archbishop set out at dawn
To the edge of Lake Constance
And once there he threw the ring
As far as he could across the water.

2

So it is that for three months now, winter months too,
The entire court of Charlemagne
Has been camped by the side of Lake Constance.

Dreaming each night of courtiers' chambers
Wineglasses lit by flames
Women warmly naked between thick cotton sheets
We wake instead to stare across gun-metal waters

And curse.

Icicles contrive a freakish music as the eastern winds migrate.

And the old man sits here at the water's edge
The gold circle of his crown upon his lap
Staring at the exact point
Where the ring disappeared.

Placebo's December

The weather wouldn't meet the will of man;
Refractory, it prismed back to hoarfrost;
A monochrome photography of winter,
Darkness latticed by bands of bitter light.

The visible spectrum had turned into an icicle.
Molecules clung together, rigidly lethargic
In the paralysed water. Placebo's mind too
Where such swift currents had flown once

Iced across now, scored with metal blades
As though skaters left hieroglyphs
For dead Egyptians. Here where he'd seen ripple
The fluent body of the whitest swimmer

Ever to beach between his blue silk sheets.
With what delight they'd snorkled, plunged,
Waving and drowning as both observed
An interchange of bodily fluids.

Bibliophile Placebo

Placebo stares in silence at his palms
Where the lines of his life describe a chaos.
Crackleware ceramics.

Now Sirius, the pestilential star appears
The dog-star bringing misery to earth.
Alexander Pope (his brother poet) dreaded it, and held his
Head the tighter
As Twickenham contracted to a migraine.
The little darkness magnified the large
As in a *camera obscura*.

Doctor Placebo considers the books on his shelves.
He has an interest (understandable surely?) in science.
He opens one at random
To find an illustration
He would rather not have found.

Lucifer Matches. Angels are bright still
Though the brightest fell.

The phossy jaw of Victorian matchworkers
Half of them under thirteen.
Chemical poisoning. Phosphorus. Not to worry:
Plenty more where they came from.
Some are born to sweet delight
Some are born to endless night.

He lifts the books out one by one and cradles them.
A collector is lost in his world of fragments
Even the fragments of misery.
Octavo, folio, duodecimo

The volumes have outgrown the house
Finding a footing on each stair and landing.

They trip him each day with mute considerations
Sometimes more real to him than his patients.

Here's *Omphalos*. Philip Gosse. 1857.
One of Placebo's treasured items.
He whispers bibliophilic endearments to its pages.

Lyell had found more time than scripture permitted.
His *Principles of Geology* suggested that the days in Genesis
Had been long days indeed.
Millions and millions of years.

And out they came then like the celebrants
In Stanley Spencer's Cookham Resurrection.
After so long in the earth.
Fossils rose from limestone, chipped and chiselled
To be cradled in the palm,
seeds from the bottom of a pharaoh's tomb,
Tricked back into life by vivid intellects
Reaching a hand through vast extinctions,
A tunnel threads the labyrinth.
Count the millennia
Inscribed in Gothic tracery
Upon a glyptodon's carapace.

Except, according to Philip Gosse, there never was a glyptodon
Merely its fossil inscribed by God
Upon the non-existent past
To make the present function.
Thus *Omphalos*, which explained that every present
Needs a past, therefore the Almighty

In fashioning Creation made a past for it.
Prochronism was the term he coined:
Things made before there was time for any making.
Though eating nothing but the dust of its extinction
Buried in the aftermath of a life not lived
The glyptodon had fluted teeth.

The Almighty being a great one for significant detail.

Darwin is staring quizzically at heaven.
He strokes his beard with such gravity and caution
You would have thought it was a pterodactyl's nest
In which fresh eggs had started breaking.

Placebo turns to the one shelf
Containing nothing but scientific papers
Each one a *punctum*.

Einstein. 1905.

Einstein. 1915.

Time's impermanence established at last.

Well, there you go.

Fittest

The moth *Biston betularia*:
A light freckled colour
Matching the surrounding trees.

Good move.

Then came the Industrial Revolution.
Trees grew darker
Highlighting such vivid flutterers for predation.
The usual random mutations produced a dark variety
Which survived the polluted environs
Till after a century 90 per cent of the moths
Where chimneys pumped out belchsmoke and dottle
Were dark.

I too am leaching darkness from the grand surround
Thinks Placebo
Though to be fair it's 4 a.m.
Midwinter.
His mirror?
Memory's polished obsidian.

Placebo Thinks Darkly of John Ruskin

A cormorant resting on the tree of life
Drying its black Gothic wings in the sun
Contemplated its forthcoming meal of flesh
As John Ruskin stared hard and contemplated the cormorant.
He swallowed finally
The words of his family Bible
Which turned immediately to wormwood inside him.

Outside the ruin that his skull contained
He saw Eden despoliated by the smoke of factories
A paradise of tin trinkets instead of fruit
Dangling from its iron branches.

And Eve with the technicolor diamond on her finger -
How long before did it lie buried
Uninflamed by any sun
Uncut, unpolished
Silent and sightless in its mineral democracy?

20th Century Elegy

As he sat on top of the moor
Riddled in the winds' rigging,
Blown on, moment to moment

Placebo thought, I'm here in the greenness
Blueness, emptiness of
Nothing but the present moment

Yet all he saw even here
Was a night-stadium sodium-lit
Whose envelope of darkness couldn't contain the cries

Placebo's Guardian Departs

Don't fly off now, Placebo thought,
Little angel assigned to my right shoulder
Ever since birth, to perch up there invisibly
These long years, me the pirate down below.
We must be sailing closer to the treasure.

That evening he turned the pages of his
Edward Lear *Illustrations of the Psittacidae*.
The splendour of those coloured wings
Rainbows iridescent in their feathers
And he recalled how Félicité in Flaubert's
'Un Coeur Simple' mistook at last her
Beloved parrot Loulou for the Holy Ghost.

Fly if you must then, he said softly.
If I had wings I'd surely join you.

Insomniac Placebo

Subject to a melancholy
Vast and formless as a fog
Doctor Placebo lies awake at dawn.

'To think is to speculate with images'. Aristotle.
Speculations. Phantasmata.
Placebo's images came out of emblem books
A dragon swallowing its own tail, for example.

Gods weightless as shadows
Their faces invisible in mirrors.

Shapes that make cats scream in the dark.

But how could he escape from history,
This melancholy vast and formless as a fog
Pressing on his mind each dawn?

Placebo's Lifeline

Time has of late been eating out of Placebo's hand.
It's down to the epidermis.
Each line maps out
A palmist's miracle.
Watch him hold on to these cryptograms
Twenty-four hours a day.

Even in sleep each line creeps
Towards its terminus.

Not in the Doctor's hands, that.

Imitation of Life

Smudged in Blue Books, grey humdrum and *grisaille*.
In the Bethlem Hospital when Richard Dadd was there
They sat in their dittos, row after row:
Replicas of one another's grief.

Placebo's Midrash

Noah while constructing his Ark from gopher wood
As the Almighty instructed
Buried all his books six feet underground
So mighty was his library
So crammed with volumes on entomology
Numismatics, dendrochronology, the unpredictable
Radioactive emissions from leaking nuclei
Even (here he hesitated) an encyclopaedia of tides
Winds, ship repair—nautical know-how.

He'd feared so many books would sink the ship.

He took note of the spot
Planning to make his bibliophile's pilgrimage back
When things around those parts were once again drier.

Sadly, the post-diluvial earth was featureless
Unless you think of feculent mud as featured
And after years of compassing, surveying,
Trigonometry geodolites
He gave up his beloved library as lost.
Had to make do now with the one book (a good one, granted)
Which had only reached Chapter Six by then
Though there was already a murder (human)
And a genocide (divine).

Things having started as they meant to go on.

Placebo Pedagogical

When Aristotle gazed on Alexander
In the temple of nymphs
The young man's head held thus, in gathering sunlight
(A Rembrandt moment)
Did he see the armies, the horses
Corpses strewn from sea to shining sea?

How inexpensive seem the mind's conquests
How blessed this world of intellectual retirement.

Ivory and gold. Prisoners and slaves.
A world is there to reach the utmost edges of.
Each night beside his knife under his soldier's pillow
The Iliad with the scholar's written emendations.
Achilles dies young.
For historical reassurance Alexander would dream
His father's assassinated body, arms and legs akimbo
On the spattered tiles.

The present and the past are one, Placebo thinks:
Both fill me with despair
The way black wine in a crystal glass
Swallows and occludes the arctic sun.

Placebo and the Entrails

Twenty-four crows once
Burnt on a funeral pyre
To show that fellow's day was truly over

Whose smoked quills
Then wrote elegies
For terminated princes

They say the feathers
Rose ten thousand feet
Blanketing black snow on Rome

Black snow, haruspicators cried,
Next week: a saltless sea, virgin Caesars
Soldiers' blades beginning to rust

Placebo's Forebear

Prometheus finding humanity full of dark forebodings
Planted in them the seeds of hope
Askew entirely to their actual condition:
The first placebo.
Then he gave them fire
Which in time they would drop from the heavens
To erase whole cities
In which their brothers and sisters resided.

This brought about a certain aggravation
In relations with the powers that be
And the onset of the titan's liverish problems.

Bonjour Placebo

Today, noticing books in the window, Doctor Placebo stepped
Inside his local charity shop
Only to find a basketful of second-hand
Brassieres, and left then, filled with *tristesse*.

Not hard to tear
A mind so fly-skinned.

One of his young female patients had a melancholy:
He diagnosed her with *tristesse*
Prescribing books he freely lent her.
Not that the books would
Lighten the *tristesse*, but they'd show
At least how many others through the centuries
Had shared it with her.

Placebo Under the Sign of Saturn

Planet of diversions and delays.
So said Walter Benjamin, born under its mighty shadow
Studying melancholia and its vast contagion
Never superseded when the humours were defrocked.

And Goya in the 1790s started to go deaf.
His bottomless depression ascribable
To Saturnism: lead-poisoning from breathing in his paints.

With the same paints in the Quinta del Sordo ten years later
He limned Saturn eating his son, so the latter couldn't grow
To kill his father.

Placebo's Last Orders

Rome ruined, heading from marble to brick
Rats and beggars sharing the streets between them
And the water, translucent in Il Duce's day,
A delivery system now for virus and bacterium
A stream of microbes jabbering and jockeying
For pole-position at the altar of a rotting carcass.

When he appears
At every street corner simultaneously
Uniformed in black, head shaven along with his chin
Grim with delight that here it is at last
The end of history, as predicted.

A dragon head protrudes from the faucet. Eyes of green mucus.
A pterodactyl lays eggs inside the morning toothpaste tube.
Last night a biplane scattered primitive explosive devices
On the Colosseum
All the more lethal for not yet being invented.
Skies flutter with leaflets penned by a minor demon
In an unknown tongue
Printed exquisitely in Gill Perpetua.

And he writes on the concrete wall with a spray-can.
He riddles the council tenement with scripts
Jagged and fragmented enough to entice interpreters.
Aramaic? Amharic? Hard to say
Since no one here this Saturday evening
Speaks a single word of either.

But they listen or half-listen anyway
And they read or half-read anyway
On their way to municipal convocations
Night-clubs with Emperor logos on washing-room tissues

Hearing in his words' finality an end-time satisfaction.
And they smile, a little fixedly, one to another.

They all of them knew it couldn't last for ever
Not with those men on squat horses
Pissing vertical squirts into hallowed ground
A matter of feet and inches from the city gates.

So let's give it one good night (best make it a long one)
Then we'll decipher those runes
Hieroglyphs, codes and encryptions
One Ogham Script fingered in granite
Slogans daubed on depilated walls and foreigners' shop windows.
Start to make plans, then.

Emblems from shadowed wings on twilit squares.

Already, ads are appearing in the military monthlies:
When each day's dawn
Turns allegorical
You know the long-awaited trouble has at last begun.

'Legionnaire. Good service record. Term of enlistment
Ending shortly. Would like to find alternative employment
Preferably far from Rome . . .'

Part Two

Ruskin and Sesame

Ruskin and Sesame

'... acting not as wealth, but (for we ought to have a correspondent term) as 'illth', causing various devastation and trouble around them ...'
  —John Ruskin, *Unto This Last*, 1860.

1

Like the man who, given radium
(A curio, a little gift, a tiny elemental)
Wore it on a silver string around his neck
And pointed out with pride this rarity
To all and sundry
Until it killed him,
Ruskin wore the rancour that he felt
For the grand machinery of fate
Turning its wheels inexorably in England;
For children working fifteen hours a day;
For ugliness emblazoned everywhere in iron;
Effie's faithlessness and Millais' malice.

Illth, he said. Written first then uttered
Before attendant crowds in lecture halls.
Illth. A moth clings to the syllable's end
Chewing holes in a gorgeous brocade
Riddled through with silk and golden thread
The length of a palace wall:
'NO WEALTH BUT LIFE.'
Illth. Furred fog of a word
Swallowing its mess of shadows
A soft-shoe-shuffle, a blur.
Bright wings mimic the rainbow
Only to sizzle in candle flame,
Such a tiny sun to die in.

There's illth.
When insect heads explode in adoration
Of the incandescent gas
One exiguous wick provides.

2

The age was steaming up.
Outside his window, industry
Re-fashioned nature in its image,
But to whose advantage exactly?
Commodities are zeroes multiplying in a ledger-book.
In lecture after lecture, he demanded
'What is wealth? What illth?
'By our art and architecture, books, music
'We'll be known, should this our name survive at all
'The great entropic principle our age is formulating…'

Railways vein the land, and snorting engines
Heave their loads up gradients. Pig iron,
Rubble for roading, tin trinkets, coal.
Out of the earth's resources, its riches
We fashion our world.

3

Sessie looks up from her book. Her parents called her
Sesame in honour of Ruskin's *Sesame and Lilies*.
She sits in Soho and sees winter light
Falling through windows to meet
Dusty air, dirty carpets
An exhausted allegory, a Dutch painting:
17th Century, each item of mundanity illuminated
As though saints' faces glowed
Bright nuclei in the oval windows of their atoms.

Her gin and tonic has dissolved its ice.
Her profile is familiar in the gloom.
Stray drinkers shuffle to the bar
Spoilt priests at a communion rail
Assessing how much faith remains to be exhausted.

Winter light.

What are we observing here, from such a distance?
A woman of a certain age and disposition
Whose breasts passed through the Bohemian
Hands of Soho
Like rations through the hands and mouths of hungry ratings
Whose thighs clutched
Torsos of painters
Sculptors, poets,
Drunks with no profession
But the Goddess Booze
A litany of foggy splendour
In veneration of befuddled dereliction.

She sees herself now as she once saw Nina Hamnett—
'Modigliani said I had the finest tits in Europe'—
Fading slowly with a glass before her
Waiting for the fellow from the BBC. Tristan.

Sesame Twilling, late child of the Twilling Shipping Line.
You will find her listed in the books as Cecil Twilling
With a note explaining how the name was really Cecilia.
But the name was really Sesame
Cut down in turn to Sessie.
She'd given up on the confusion years before
Becoming simply Cecil Twilling
For all official purposes. Why not?
(Some thought it the argot of an ancient dyke)

But to herself she was and always would be Sessie.
Now Sessie awaited Tristan.

Her semi-abstract paintings
Exhibited, reproduced, admired throughout the 50s
By Herbert Read, Ben Nicholson and Barbara Hepworth.
Francis had said nothing
In all the hours she'd spent with him at Muriel's
Staring into the eyes of one stone god or another
As the champagne pinked its bubbles
And words ballooned.
But Francis, she knew, thought little enough of anyone
Still living and holding a brush,
Apart from a few like Lucian and of course himself.
Even Jackson Pollock was no more than 'the lacemaker'
The dynamic threading of his drips condemning him
To the millinery section of a haberdasher's shop.

Sessie knew that she'd done something
Still could on certain days
When her hands weren't trembling
In her tiny attic studio in Highgate.
She'd had a fragment of the vision bequeathed her—
Few enough do, and she knew it.
So now she waited.
For Tristan from the BBC.
A third her age.
Who modelled his brain for the camera
As though this mind might strut nude and enticing,
A Plato lap-dancing before his avid patrons.

Illth. When a steam engine shouted
It used to make that sound
                    however briefly.

Illth illth illth. Right up the gradient
Towards the summit.

Ever onwards and upwards:
Her father, the shipping magnate
Sir Thomas had been keen on
Climbing every mountain.
He'd disinherited her at twenty-one
When word got back to Twilley House in Bucks
(His own armorial device on the gates,
A trifle gaudy, she'd always thought)
How many boho bucks had been riding the family maiden.
Ah, those were the days. Who needed eminence?
Give me back my body, Sessie thought.
My body, my verve, my bonding boys.
I came up with a strategy to deal with them:
Whenever they jumped me, I jumped right back.
Some stopped there and then
Astounded at such symmetry.

Ben Nicholson took Cubism and made it pastoral
Softened its diagrammatic edges
Transmuted it to English pastel and topography.

An alchemical process dependent on curious distillations
Afforded by the Cornish coast, climatic metamorphoses
A mathematical approach to nature
And the primitive panache of Alfred Wallis
Old sailor home from the sea
Filling his scraping boards with colour
Hearing the devil farting down his chimney every evening.
Ben looked and saw what art should be:
A spectrum of delight in nature, minus affectation.
Her own view entirely.
She spent two years down there in Cornwall with them

Was even taken one night by a poet in Zennor
In a field laid with frost while a motionless goat looked on.
Next day she was too hung-over to recall whether or not
She'd called out in pleasure. All she remembered
Was green and white, grass, frost, and that motionless goat
His eyes tiny beacons in the darkness
                    (vertical, verdant flares)
A heroic fumbling through duffel, wool
And dark wooden buttons.
So where then is Tristan? Is he parting at last from Isolde?
Maybe they too are spreadeagled in a Cornish field.
That would explain the delay in getting started.

4

Here is Ruskin on rust in Tunbridge Wells in 1858.

It's richer than gold, and a better provider
We could litanize
The life of metals with the breath put into them,
For the breath of life in Genesis is oxygen
As well as *ruah* or *pneuma*—
The ochreous stain on the marble is a form of beauty.
Your eyes should fill with salt each time you see
Iron in a state of rust.

Only one metal which will not rust readily
And that has caused Death rather than Life;
It will not be put to its right use till it is made
A pavement of, and so trodden under foot.

The family gold had been denied to Sessie
Whatever coin she'd had she made herself.
Never a fashionable painter, if greatly admired.
Now out of fashion entirely.

Coniston Water darkens
When the mood of the weather turns tragic
(Ruskin invented the term 'pathetic fallacy')
As though recalling how transient are all things
Including the atmosphere of one small blue-veined planet.
And from the house at the lake's edge if you listen closely
                    you will shortly hear a scream.

5

In 1819 the Reverend William Buckland was appointed
Oxford's first Professor of Geology.
His house, which Ruskin visited, contained his specimens,
Many still alive. There you might hear the rumbling of the bear,
The jackal's hungry keening, and eat from a menu
Rare in Oxford at the time. Among the *plats du jour:*
Battered dormouse and a crocodile sautée.
All the while animals moaned, cried out
In steerage, as though they were still on the Ark
With a drowned world rolling in the dark beneath them.
Not as loud, though, as Rossetti's menagerie on Cheyne Walk
Where Swinburne and the monkeys out-gibbered
                    one another nightly.
All these cries entered Ruskin's mind. Years later
In madness in Brantwood
                    at the edge of Coniston Water
Such voices would be
Ventriloquised by Satan at greater volume.

By then they wouldn't scare, those creatures from Saint Anthony's
Apocalypse. None of his screams could budge
His shape-shifting tormentors so much as an inch.

6

Tristan arrives at last. A pretty boy, no doubt of that.
Did Nature do his hair
Or is coiffure required to put a little curl
           right in the middle of his forehead?
Years before she'd most likely have had him.
Years? Decades more like. And he's flirtatious too.
After twenty minutes with a camera hovering
           hither and thus between them
She realises with a thump that the programme is not really
About artists she knew,
Like Nicholson and Hepworth,
And their relation to her own life's work
As she'd been told (however vaguely)
In the phone-call.
But instead the theme is anecdote and gossip,
The usual suspects from Soho and Fitzrovia.
'I think I'd like another drink,' she says. 'A double.'
Tristan proffers his charm as though it should prove
Sustenance enough for any arty dowager.
Thus with his winsome smile:
'You only slept with Dylan once, I think, but you must have
Met him many times before and after.'
Ah yes, the Welsh boy, Celtic
Waves poured smoothly
Into a decanter of cut-glass BBC urbanity.
She could still remember vividly enough.
No distinction earned in sleeping once with Dylan;
More trouble not to.
She takes a steady drink and feels the gin break through.

'My name's not really Cecil.'
'Cecilia, isn't it?'
'No, Sesame, in fact. As in *Sesame and Lilies*, a work you know,

I'm sure.
Why did Ruskin take to political economy, Tristan?
As odd, as troubling in its way as Ezra Pound adopting economics
For a theme. 1860. *Unto This Last.*
He even invented a word to try to describe the nightmare
We inhabit: illth. Not wealth but illth.
Now Soho when I knew it was an escape from illth.
We made no trinkets here, though a few
Sold their bodies—quite a bargain basement, this place.
When Ruskin ranted about
The Great Exhibition of 1851, all those commodities
Parading themselves under steel and glass
          like tremulous bodies
All the gewgaws, the gimcrack pleasantries
Of mass production, while paintings were rotting
At that very moment in the rain in Venice
After the Austrian bombardments,
He was pointing us all to a future in Soho.
You will keep this in, won't you, love?'
(He nods and she knows he is lying).

'Here you see we only cared for what deserved our caring.
We painted, we wrote, made music, stole,
We didn't pay taxes, and yes, I grant you, young man,
Now and then we made love, but who doesn't? Your programme
Should try to explain how for half a mile around
These parts we fled the illth and tried to find true wealth
In one another's company, one another's paintings,
One another's arms.'

Later back at the BBC with a listless crew, Tristan shrugs
To his producer:
'Bugger all, I should think.
Old bint just kept banging on about John Ruskin.'

7

Sessie sits in the back of the taxi
Taking her to Highgate
And lifts from her bag
An olive-green volume
Published in 1891
By George Allen of Sunnyside, Orpington
And 8, Bell Yard, Temple Bar, London.
Sesame and Lilies by John Ruskin, LL.D.
Already the twelfth edition in the original form.
Inscribed thus: *To My Darling Sesame,*
When others ask why you weren't named more predictably—
Marigold perhaps or Daisy or Rose—
Show them this rarity of prose.

With all my love, Father.

Sir Thomas. How she would like to meet him again now.
But then maybe she'd do that, shortly.

When she climbs unsteadily from the cab
She pays first, tipping too heavily
Then holds the book up to the driver's face.
'I was born inside that, you know.'

'Good for you, love. Take care up them stairs now.'

She wished Henrietta were still around.
Sessie would have said, 'All I wanted
Was to talk about my work,
While I still have a tongue in my head forming words.
All he wanted was to talk about
The size of Dylan Thomas's todger.'

Henrietta would have roared, as she frequently did
And poured them both another massive drink.

She lay on the bed and looked around her
At her paintings on the wall.
They were good, all of them. She knew that.
She couldn't have lived with them otherwise.

Ruskin's bed in Brantwood was surrounded
By Turner prints
Which hallucinated come night-time
Into demons shrieking.
Henrietta would have calmed him down
Pressing his head to her breast
(she bore little resemblance to Rose la Touche
as Bacon's paintings
or Deakin's porno shots make clear—
No anorexic, she).

'Poor Johnny,' she'd have said. 'Poor John.'

Sessie switches on the tiny television in the corner.
A black man and a white man chatting.
'How come you guys can sing so high when it suits you?'
'Must be all those centuries of white guys
Like you kicking us in the balls, man.'
'So that would explain your total lack of interest in sex
These days then, Harry.'
The laughter continues as she switches off the set.

'Open Sesame,' Dylan had said
On learning her name
One Fitzrovian night filled with so much
Porter and ice-cream even she

Had thought the world might be
Entirely black and white.

But morning was grey
Such a limbo of shadows sashaying
It seemed the Underworld
Had launched its ad. campaign.

And in the dark that night an engine panting
Illth illth illth
Is climbing its way to Coniston Water
Where the fish have already stopped dreaming.
An old man with hoarfrost on his head
And a Gothic rib-cage
Crouching naked in the corner of his room
Falls silent at last.

Part Three

Labyrinth and Trivium

Labyrinth

Ariadne

My brother the monster. You'll recall.

My mother, Queen Pasiphaë, being no better than she should have been, fell for the white bull. He was a most attractive creature, but even so.

The cunning old courtier Daedalus is called in. She wants the white bull inside her.
So he builds her a cow from wood, big enough for her to climb inside, as though she were a Greek soldier and this were Troy. And there's an aperture on the underside large enough for the pizzle of a taurus to intrude and squirt out the future.

The deed is performed under cover of darkness.

Ariadne, they say, you have a little brother, dear.

The body looked fair enough, but the head, as you'll recall, was that of a bull. A handsome bull, it's true. Even so.

When Theseus arrived I gave him my heart before he'd even come into focus. Blame the gods for this. We blame them for everything else. That's my mother's alibi in regard to the white bull. A curse from a disgruntled deity. Poseidon. The usual story.

Those young men and women shipped over in boatloads to sate my brother's cravings had caused consternation. There'd been a commotion in the press. St George and the Dragon all over again, or perhaps that was still to come.
If you go in there you'll never come out I tell him, but look at this. Just look at this.

To hold the bull in place while he was covering my mother, Daedalus had made the finest, strongest, whitest thread you ever did see. Never would say what it was made of, but you could bobbin it out for miles, then clew it all back in. I had caught fish with it; once even lassoed an albatross. The bird's neck was broken by the time I'd winched it back.

Take this with you. I'll stay outside. And when you are done with your business in there I'll wind you back in; all the way back until we are belly to belly.
I heard the great cry and knew that was the last one he'd ever make. Felt something die in me too, however tiny it was. He was my half-brother after all. Little Horns, I'd called him. Then Theseus came back out of the dark tunnel towards me. I felt the distance between us shortening as my breathing grew quicker.

He took me away, as agreed. But what came next had not been agreed: he dumped me on the first island we came to, which was Naxos. A woman who had betrayed her own family. What decent girl would do that? Daughter of a bull's whore, and almost certainly no better than she should be. I could hear him laughing as he told the story to his sailors. One final use for the thread, then. I knotted it firmly to the branch and put the noose around my neck.

Could still see his boat vanishing on the horizon during my final twitches of life.

Now I live on in the skies, if live is the right word to use here.

Pasiphaë

A curse is like a sea around you, swelling and ebbing, stinging your eyes with its salt. Particularly when the curse comes from Poseidon, who is the sea.

The white bull should have been sacrificed, but my dear husband Minos was smitten. Smitten with the beauty of the beast. And so was I. Then when Poseidon's curse arrived, it was more than being smitten. He filled my mind. Filled my dreams. I was a meadow with him riding over me.

Daedalus asked what the old man would do. I told him he wanted it too. Wanted a son so strong no foreign invader would ever dare set foot on Crete. And so he built it, constructed a shape cunning enough to look like a beautiful cow. And I was the white cow with the white bull inside me. When he came it was the seven seas, the thrash of Poseidon all the way to my womb.

And then our boy, our bull-boy. Minotaurus. Half him; half me. Strong enough, that's for sure. I think I might be the inventor of disenchantment for you all, because nothing was ever quite the same after that. No man arriving with his little wand could bring back the magic of that night in the fields with my splendid bull.

He wanted children. He is a god of generation, after all, at least according to the peasants round these parts who, despite their credulity, are often right. But like the mule, he was made from a miscegenation of species, and like the mule he was sterile. So we brought him children, boys and girls from Athens. Every year we brought them to him.

When Theseus was done with his butchery in there, and had taken my whore of a daughter with him to the next island, they came out, one by one, the Athenian children. Something in their eyes had brightened to counter the darkness of the labyrinth. And it has never entirely gone, the light awash in their eyes. I visit them each day in the little chapel we made for them, down by the seashore, where Poseidon listens to their liturgies.

In my old age with my old king (who's not touched me for years) I find myself wondering if that boy had horns at all. Did he not just shout a little more than other boys, throw things about the place (even courtiers sometimes) making everyone in palace rooms uncomfortable, until we agreed, my husband and I, that he really needed a home of his own? I know, Minos said, let's call it an asylum.

Minotaur

All I could do was one thing after another, until it was accomplished.

What was accomplished?

I was made out of other people's desires, until Theseus finally had his.

Is it like this for all of you?

Theseus

I was meant to take down the black sail and hoist the white and I forgot. So my father threw himself to his death over the cliff.

And I have had a black sail in my mind catching the dark wind of the future ever since.

(I heard that she hanged herself on Naxos. No need for that. Poseidon would have explained, if she'd let him: plenty more fish in the sea, little sister. There were plenty more where I came from.)

Trivium

Silenus to Midas: 'Don't get born. Or if you do, die the minute you can thereafter.'

Three lines were drawn on the day of his birth.

Like the lines that crease your palm.

Laius was one, Jocasta the other, he was the third.

Then the blind man led by the boy came along and declared that these three lines already formed a knot so tight that one of them must be strangled by it.

So they sent the boy to the hills to die, three days after he was born.

But kindness is hard to banish entirely, even in the ghetto; even in the mountains.
So this third line, the line of banishment and exile, the line of infanticide (the refusal of the future) continued mapping time out. And one day it came back to meet the riddling melodic keening of the Sphinx. The city was saved and they gave him for a queen Jocasta.

The three lines had already met once more by then, since they had never been untangled.

At the trivium, where the three roads meet outside Delphi, one line had met another, Oedipus met Laius and killed him. He killed the past there and then as Laius had attempted to kill the future. But the third road led back from the murdered father to the widowed mother, and back to the knot of the prophecy.

'We give her to you as your queen.'

This for answering the Sphinx's riddle.

What creature walks on four legs in infancy, two in maturity, three in old age?

Me, said Oedipus. I am the answer to the murderous riddle. Three roads, this trinity of states, all meet in me.

On four legs alone in the mountain until the shepherd took pity.

On two legs now, staring into the blank but somehow whimsical eyes of the future.

And tomorrow . . .

Jocasta washed the sheets she had shared the night before with the king. She would let no maidservants touch them.

That evening on being told the news she tied them together into a rope and hanged herself.

And Oedipus left the city, led by his daughters, leaning on a stick. The city he had left on four legs, and ruled on two, he now left on three. What he saw he saw with no eyes, having blinded himself to be rid of the world's vision.

Three lives. Three roads.

The trivial intersection.

Oedipus

I answered her once, and she died. What is the riddle? The riddle is me. Four legs two legs three legs. Kicking my way out of a woman's body.

And then the other woman understood the riddle too and died. That I, whose little legs had once been bound together, had walked back on two legs into her life. And when I climbed between her thighs there were four legs again. Such a homecoming. Pushing back into the body I came out of. The house, like so many classical houses, was furnished with black terror. It must have been from us, I think, that Goya lifted his ideas for interior decoration at the Quinto. Black paintings in the curtained house.

Now only three legs again. Tap tap tapping my way blindly out of Thebes, led by the children who came out from between her legs, as I did once. Ah my sisters, who are also my daughters. My eyes can no longer see what my body did back there. A blessing, that. I have become a seer at last.

I who had one eye too many
Now have none
Unfit for the sun to see
Who will never see the sun again.

Drawn to the ecstatic zone
A questioning female face
(even her lion paws looked warm
her claws could surely scratch so lovingly)
I am drawn back to that rocky promontory
Where she once stared down

A raptor needing birdflesh
   A lion needing a kill
   A symmetric winged question soaring

A fighter plane already spinning down
Above Kentish farmfields circa 1940.

You look and look for the parachute opening
Whichever uniform the pilot might be wearing.

Jocasta

When the old hand on my breast was replaced by the young one, I opened my stirring thighs to let the future in. But it was the past that arrived, as always, and with such urgency.

The future already coiled inside it.

We all died the day he was born. We died as we read the prophecy written in his eyes. And he didn't even blink. *Nefas*.

Sphinx

The question once answered, the plague is lifted.

For now.
The crops grow round Thebes like tribes of vernal salutation.

My smile, sinister and beguiling, has gone underground with Persephone.

But I was only ever the bearer of the question, not its begetter. A mouth, no more. A mouth with a lion's body, a woman's face;

wings those of a bat under a microscope. The sun never sets eyes on a shadow.

With me gone, Oedipus became the question he himself had answered.
He replied to the woman's question, but he'd not yet heard the woman's reply.
One death. Two. Bad manners to count.

Soon there'll be more, all the same.

Take care with those questioners perched high above rocky valleys. Find a plain to enter, if you must enter Thebes. Any plain. Keep everything level. That's the way the gods prefer it. The female's question can never be brought down to earth.

Anagnorisis

I turned up to deliver the good news. How delighted he would be, that troubled King.

His father dead. How could a son not rejoice to find that the old man was dead, and he'd never had to kill him after all?

So the Oracle's prediction that he'd kill his own progenitor, then sleep with his mother, couldn't be true, now could it?

Everything was fine. Just as long as he was who he thought he was.

And in the silence through which he stared at me I had long enough to start to ponder something: which of us is precisely who he thinks he is?

Which hero in heaven or on earth has ever exhibited that rare distinction?

Footnote

James Frazer in *The Golden Bough* had treated myth as though it were a first clumsy gesture towards science. Wittgenstein protested: 'This is too big to be a mistake.' But Freud did something even more radical. He decided that the myth knew more than the science of his day. The myth of Oedipus had expressed a truth, as allegory, that science itself could not countenance. The myth expressed a universal desire which the conscious mind had attempted to expunge.

Freud saw performances in Paris and Vienna and was struck by the powerful impact the drama had on a contemporary audience. Why? Why should these bizarre goings-on from two and a half millennia before have any impact at all, except for curious antiquarians? Why should the unique horrors affect anyone at all so powerfully? What buried tangle of desires and inhibitions was being unearthed? Thus it began—the elaboration of what we now call the Oedipus Complex.

This had a curious result: the psychoanalyst became the figure of Oedipus, riddling a way through the darkness of the Sphinx's questions, refusing to be halted in such a dangerous enquiry. Freud even had his bookplate designed with an image of Oedipus confronting the Sphinx. The text proclaimed that Oedipus was a strong man; one prepared to confront the riddle. The analyst, like the King of Thebes himself, was one who was prepared to peer into the darkness. The allegorical forms through which the human mind channelled its unspeakable desire had to be translated into science by a modern priesthood of suspicion. But might this involve a self-elected blindness?

Hölderlin had translated *Oedipus Rex* and insisted that the true crime, the unforgivable trespass of the riddle-solver, had in fact been to stare into the darkness of the gods and see too much. *Nefas* was the word given to this prying by any human into the cauldron of secrets reserved for divinity alone. Like Prometheus's theft of fire from the gods, *nefas* was a stealing of knowledge which only the gods were permitted to possess. By then Hölderlin was already on his way to the tower at Tübingen, and a life of mental alienation. Most of his contemporaries thought his version of the Oedipus plays was merely one more sign of his insanity. But then Freud in old age would often refer to his daughter Anna as Antigone. And if London was the Colonus of his exile, after such blinding revelations, one must note that he was always photographed there with a stick in his hand.

www.ingramcontent.com/pod-product-compliance
Lightning Source LLC
Chambersburg PA
CBHW031200160426
43193CB00008B/451